11-21-11

11-16-11

Boa Constrictor

By Cede Jones

Gareth Stevens
Publishing

Please visit our Web site, www.garethstevens.com. For a free color catalog of all our high-quality books, call toll free 1-800-542-2595 or fax 1-877-542-2596.

Library of Congress Cataloging-in-Publication Data

Jones, Cede.
Boa constrictor / Cede Jones.
    p. cm. — (Killer snakes)
Includes bibliographical references and index.
ISBN 978-1-4339-4536-6 (pbk.)
ISBN 978-1-4339-4537-3 (6-pack)
ISBN 978-1-4339-4535-9 (library binding)
1. Boa constrictor—Juvenile literature. I. Title.
QL666.O63J66 2011
597.96'7—dc22

                                    2010024475

First Edition

Published in 2011 by
Gareth Stevens Publishing
111 East 14th Street, Suite 349
New York, NY 10003

Copyright © 2011 Gareth Stevens Publishing

Designer: Michael J. Flynn
Editor: Greg Roza

Photo credits: Cover, pp. 1, (2–4, 6–8, 10, 12, 14, 16–18, 20–24 snake skin texture), 5, 11, 15, 16–17, 21 Shutterstock.com; pp. 6–7, 13 iStockphoto.com; p. 9 Tim Laman/National Geographic/Getty Images; p. 19 Yuri Cortez/AFP/Getty Images.

Printed in the United States of America

CPSIA compliance information: Batch #CW11GS: For further information contact Gareth Stevens, New York, New York at 1-800-542-2595.

Contents

Boldface words appear in the glossary.

Meet the Boa Constrictor

Boa constrictors are large snakes that live in Central and South America. They are good swimmers, but they like to stay on dry land. They can also climb trees. During the day, boa constrictors sleep inside empty trees or holes in the ground. They hunt at night.

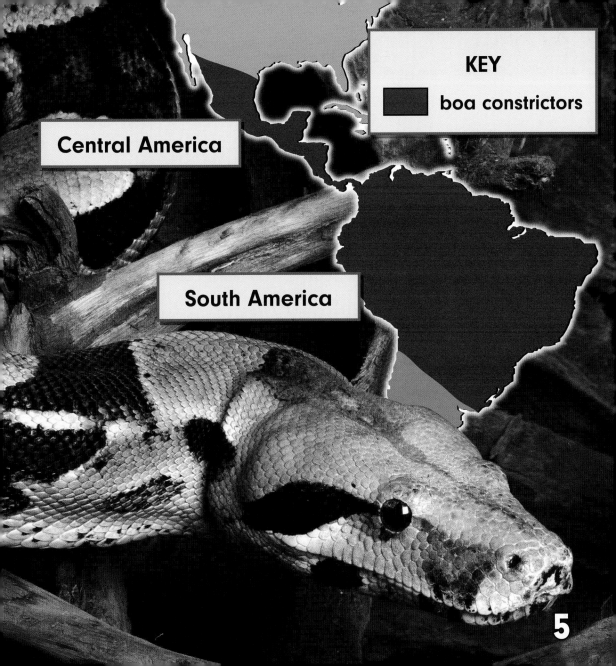

Central America

South America

KEY
boa constrictors

5

Most adult boa constrictors are between 8 and 10 feet (2.4 and 3 m) long and weigh about 60 pounds (27 kg). However, they can grow up to 13 feet (4 m) long and weigh about 100 pounds (45 kg)! Females are usually larger than males.

Made for Hunting

Boa constrictors are made for hunting. They have colors and markings that help them hide. They can be shades of brown, red, green, yellow, and black. Blending into its surroundings allows a boa to surprise its **prey**.

9

The boa constrictor's tongue is like your nose. It can sense odors. By sticking out its tongue, the boa constrictor can "smell" nearby prey. The boa constrictor has special parts around its mouth that sense heat. This helps the boa constrictor find prey in the dark.

Give Me a Hug

Have you ever been hugged so hard you couldn't breathe? That's what a boa constrictor's hug feels like! Boa constrictors kill prey by wrapping their long bodies around the prey and **squeezing**. This is how they got their name. "Constrict" is another word for "squeeze."

Let's Eat!

A boa constrictor eats almost anything it can catch, including pigs, lizards, birds, and monkeys. First, it grabs an animal with its teeth. Then, it wraps its body around the animal and squeezes until the prey can't breathe. Some boa constrictors hold an animal underwater until it drowns.

15

Once a boa constrictor's prey is dead, it's time to eat. A boa constrictor's upper and lower **jaws** can pull apart. This allows the snake to open its mouth really wide. The boa constrictor doesn't chew its food. It swallows the meal whole!

17

Baby Boas

Female boa constrictors give birth to as many as 60 babies at one time. Newborn boa constrictors are between 14 and 22 inches (36 and 56 cm) long. They start hunting right away. Young boa constrictors eat small **rodents**, such as mice and rats.

Boa Constrictors and People

Many people think boa constrictors attack people, but they don't. Some people keep them as pets! In some places, boa constrictors are valued because they kill pests such as mice and rats. They are sometimes hunted for their skins and for food.

Snake Facts
Boa Constrictor

Length	usually 8 to 10 feet (2.4 to 3 m) long up to 13 feet (4 m)
Weight	up to 100 pounds (45 kg)
Where It Lives	Central and South America
Life Span	20 to 30 years
Killer Fact	Boa constrictors have hooked teeth. They curve backwards! This helps boas hold on to their prey while wrapping their bodies around the meal.

Glossary

jaw: the upper or lower part of the mouth

prey: an animal caught and eaten by another animal

rodent: a small, furry animal with large front teeth, such as a mouse

squeeze: to press something tightly

For More Information

Books

Gunderson, Megan M. *Boa Constrictors.* Edina, MN: ABDO Publishing, 2011.

Sexton, Colleen. *Boa Constrictors.* Minneapolis, MN: Bellwether Media, 2010.

Web Sites

Boa Constrictors

kids.nationalgeographic.co.in/kids/animals/creaturefeature/boa/

Read more about boa constrictors and see photos of the snake.

Reptiles: Boa

www.sandiegozoo.org/animalbytes/t-boa.html

Read about the differences between boas, pythons, and anacondas.

Index